MY FIRST LEARNING ALPHABET

알파벳 연습장

A a Pick an apple!

Look and stick the letter A and a.

A is for 🍎 apple.

● Read and write.

● Draw a line following the letter A and a.

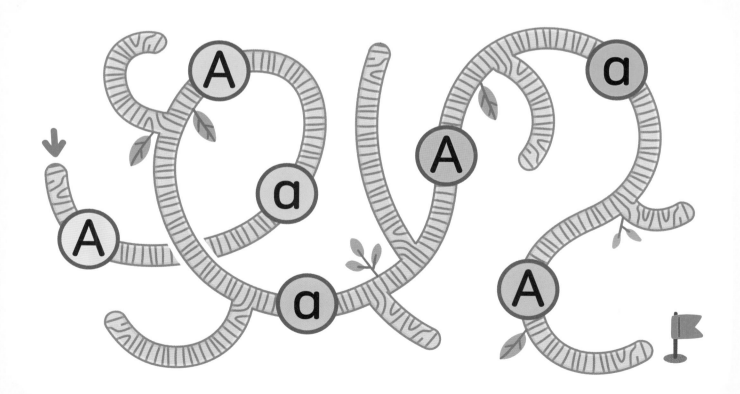

Bb Dancing butterflies

Look and color the butterflies, purple for B and yellow for b.

B is for 🦋 butterfly.

● Read and write.

B B B

b b b

● Draw a line following the letter B and b.

Cc Happy birthday to you!

Look and stick the letter C and c.

C is for  cake.

● Read and write.

C C C C

c c c

● Circle the letter C and c.

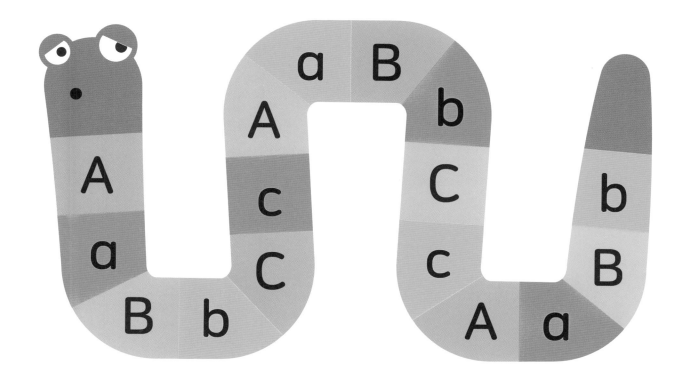

Dd

Look at the duck family.

Look and stick the letter D and d.

D is for duck.

• Read and write.

• Circle the letter D and d.

A a d C
c   D
D C B a
b   b
b C d A B

Ee

Hi, my babies.

Look and stick the letter E and e.

E is for egg.

● Read and write.

E E E E

e e e e

● Match the correct big letter and small letter.

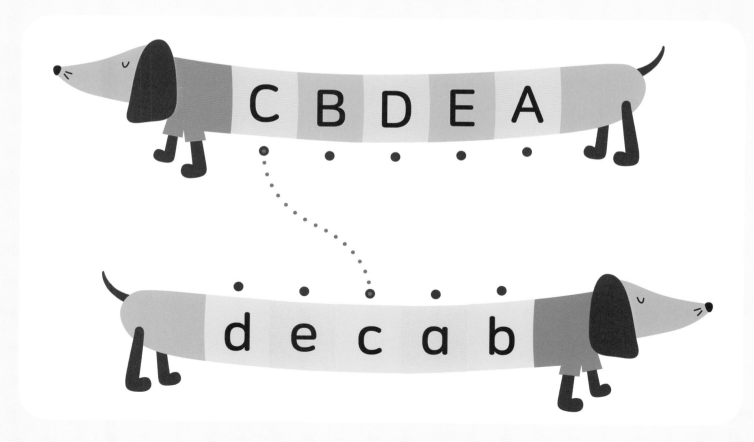

C B D E A

d e c a b

Ff Jump, jump, Frog.

Circle and follow the letter F and f for helping the baby frog to meet his mom.

F is for  frog.

- Read and write.

F F F

f f f

- Circle the letter F and f.

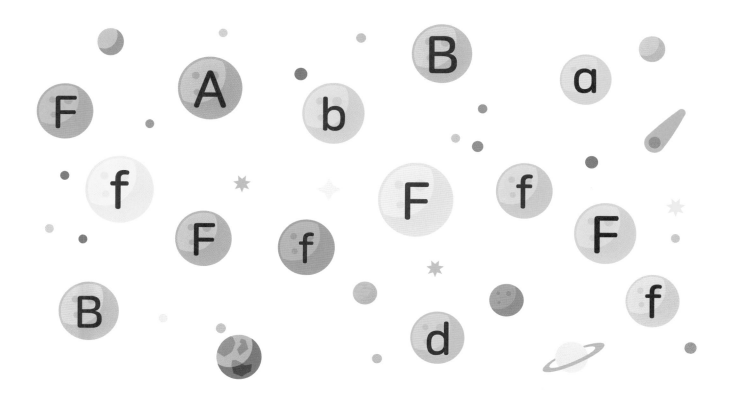

Gg

Long neck giraffes

Look and stick the letter G and g.

G is for giraffe.

● Read and write.

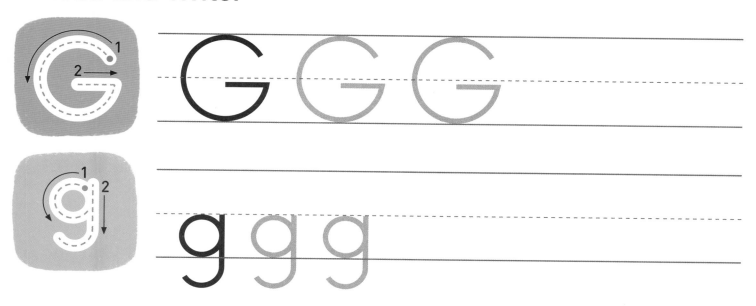

● Circle the letter G and g.

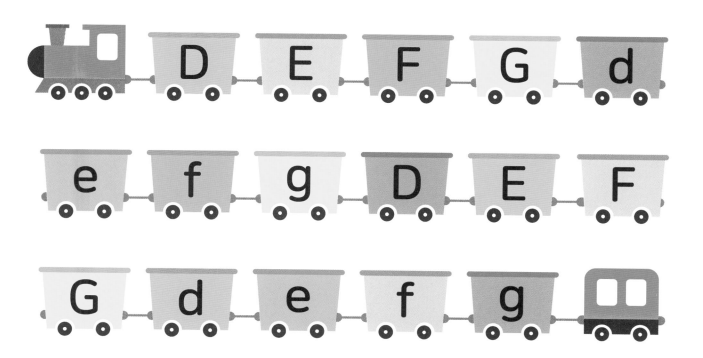

Hh

Hats for sale!

Look and stick the letter H and h.

H is for  hat.

• **Read and write.**

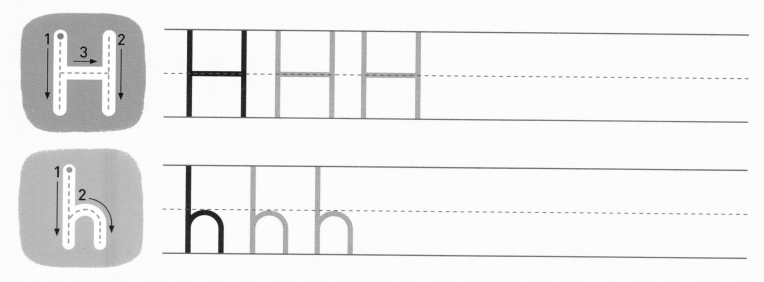

• **Find and circle the correct letter to match.**

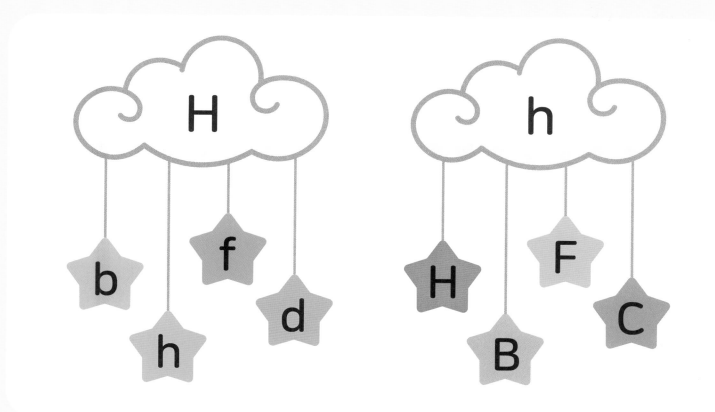

I i

I love ice cream.

Look and color the ice cream, pink for I and blue for i.

ICE CREAM

I is for 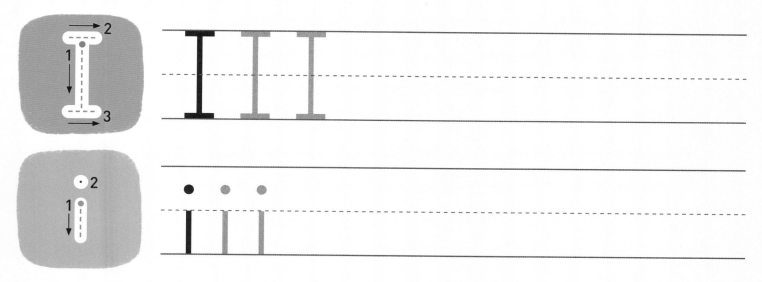 ice cream.

• Read and write.

• Circle the letter I and i.

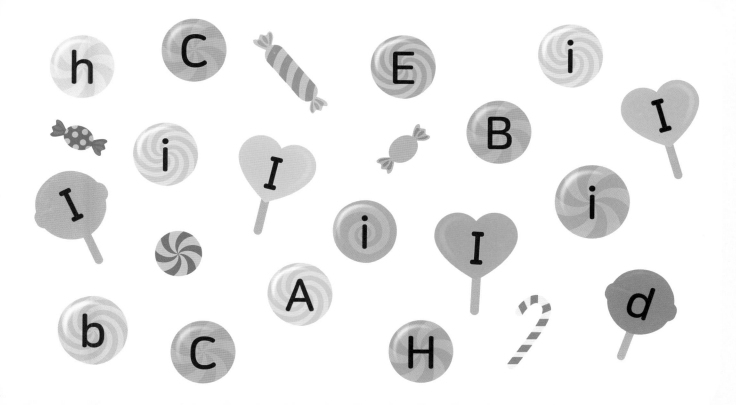

Jj

Hang your jackets side by side.

Look and stick the letter J and j.

20

J is for jacket.

- Read and write.

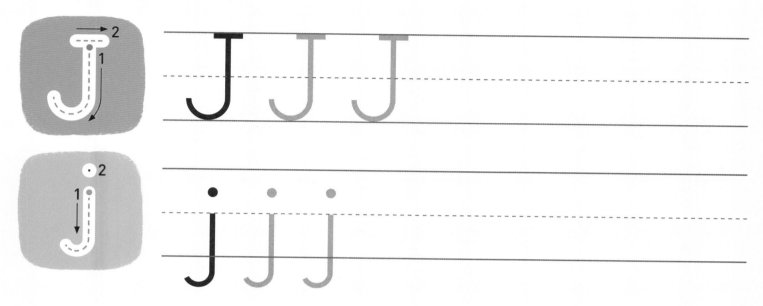

- Draw a line following the letter J and j dot to dot.

Kk

Fly, fly high.

Look and stick the letter K and k.

K is for  kite.

● Read and write.

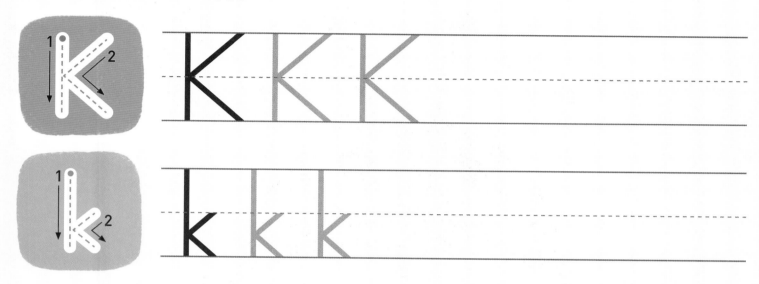

● Draw a line following the K and k.

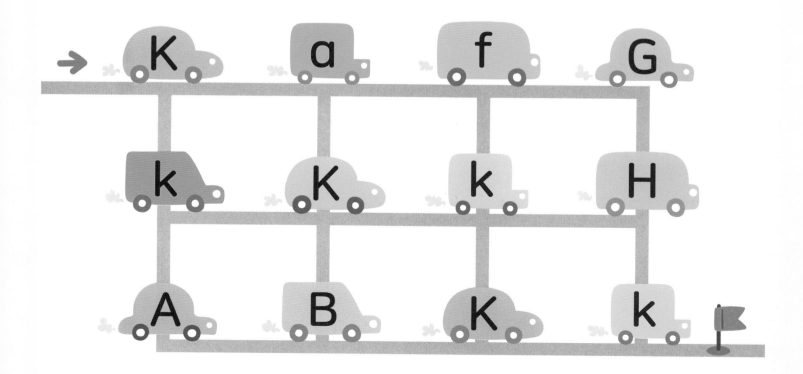

Ll

How many black spots?

Look and color the ladybird, red for L and black for l.

L is for ![ladybird] ladybird.

• **Read and write.**

• **Circle the letter L and l.**

Mm Let's drink some milk!

Look and stick the letter M and m.

M is for  milk.

● Read and write.

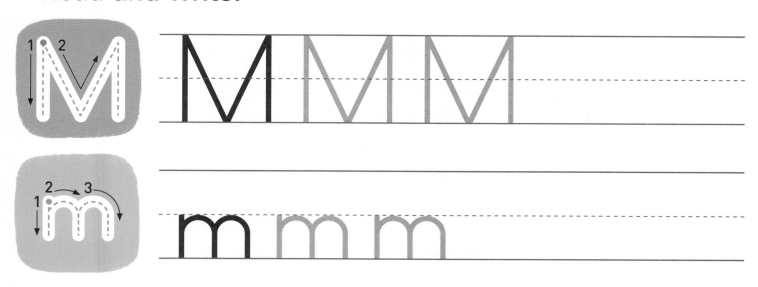

● Match the correct big letter and small letter.

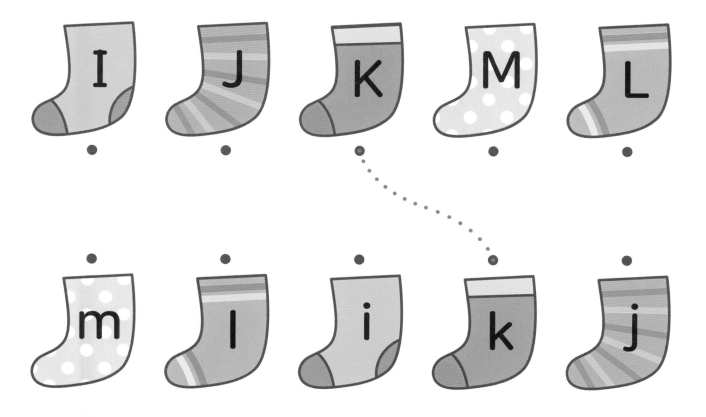

Nn Meet a friend.

Draw a line following the letter N and n.

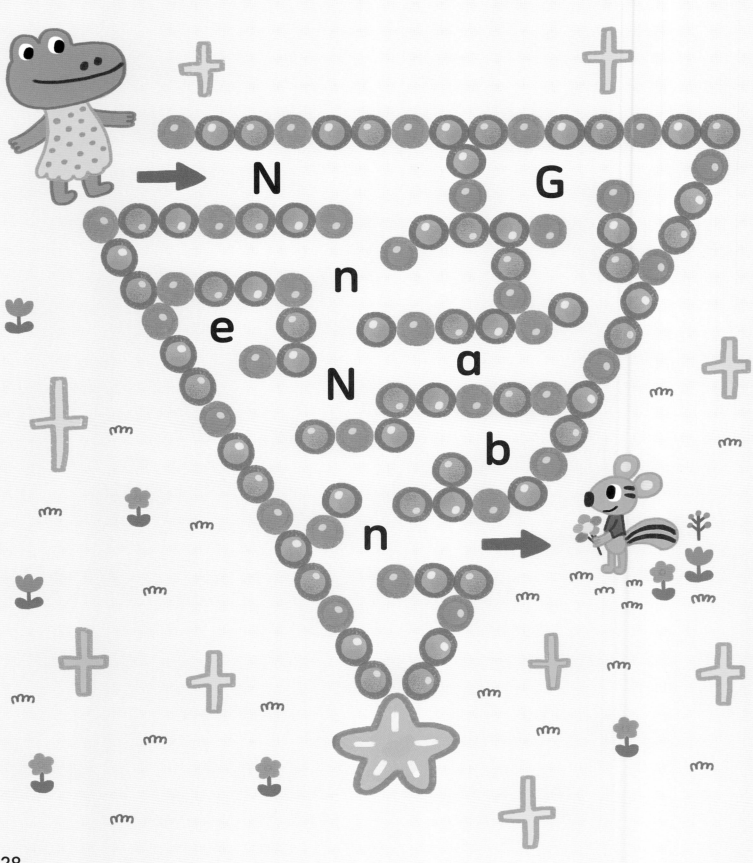

N is for necklace.

• **Read and write.**

• **Circle the letter N and n.**

Oo

Juggle, juggle fruits.
Look and stick the letter O and o.

O is for 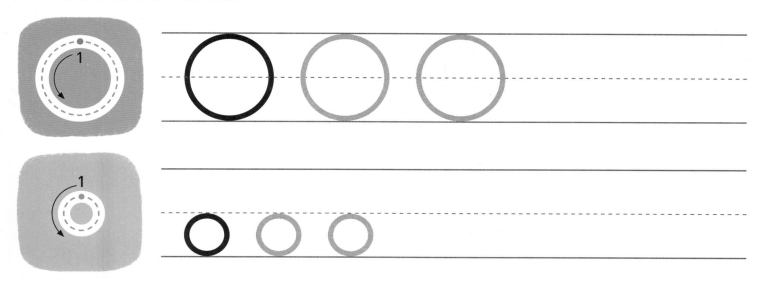 orange.

- Read and write.

- Circle the letter O and o.

n i L i o H

N O H H

h n o L h

Pp Let's make a jack-o-lantern.

Look and stick the letter P and p.

P

p

P is for 🎃 pumpkin.

● Read and write.

● Draw a line following the letter P and p from start.

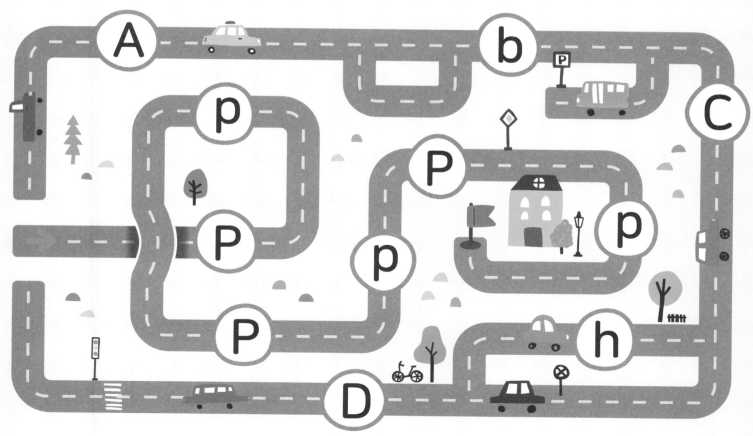

Qq

Hello, beautiful Queen.

Look and stick the letter Q and q.

Q is for queen.

- Read and write.

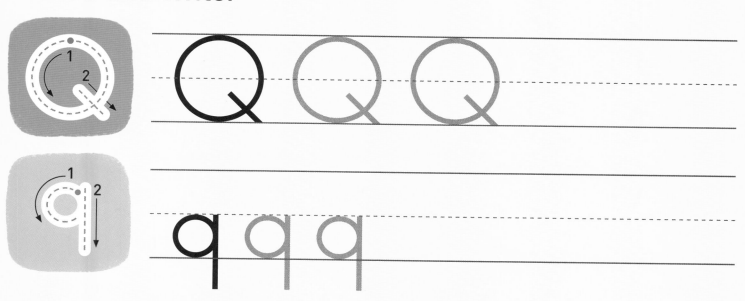

- Circle the letter Q and q.

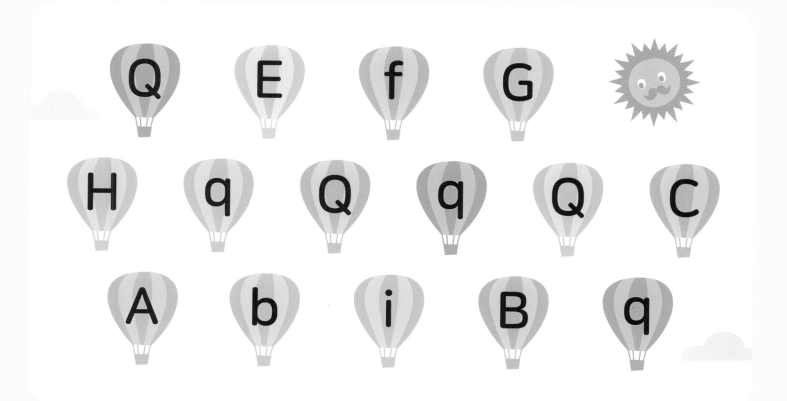

Rr Let's make a robot.

Look and stick the letter R and r.

R is for  robot.

● Read and write.

R R R R

r r r r

● Circle the letter R and r.

N O P R

R n o

r q r m

Ss Party day! Put on the skirt.

Look and stick the letter S and s.

S is for  skirt.

- Read and write.

S S S

s s s

- Match the correct big letter and small letter.

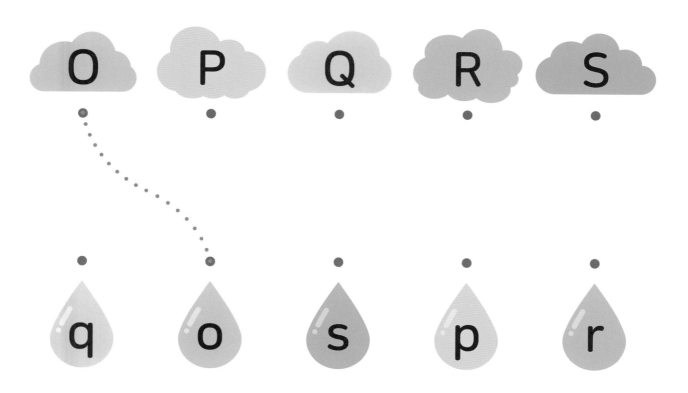

O P Q R S

q o s p r

Tt Under the sea

Look and stick the letter T and t.

T is for 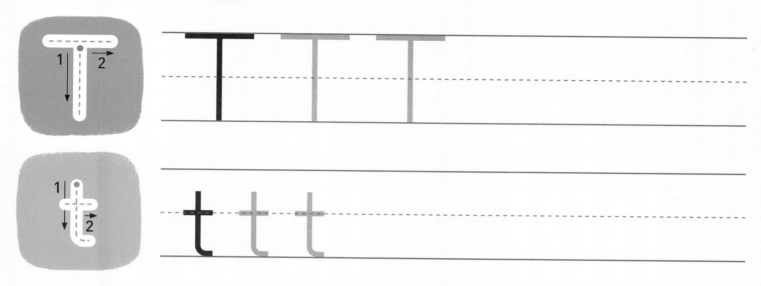 turtle.

● Read and write.

● Find and circle the letter T or t.

Uu Share my umbrella.

Look and stick the letter U and u.

U is for 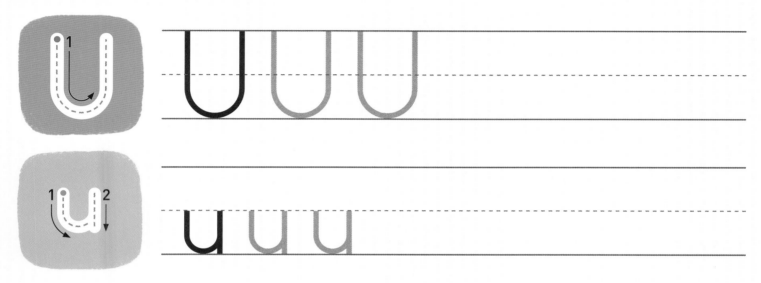 umbrella.

- Read and write.

- Draw a line following U and u from start to finish.

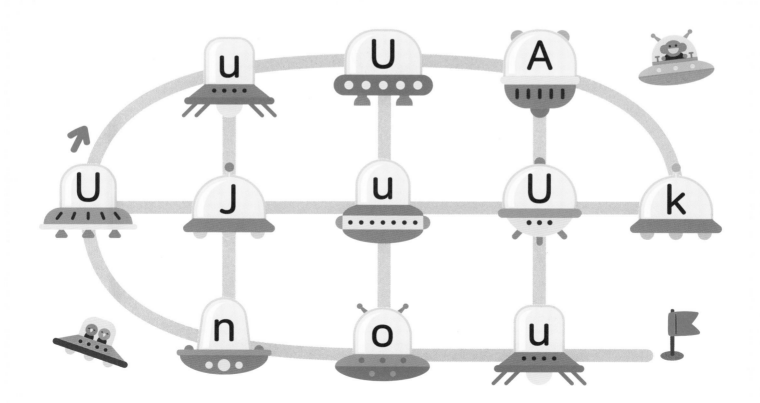

Vv Ready to listen?

Look and stick the letter V and v.

V is for  violin.

- Read and write.

- Draw a line following V and v from start to finish.

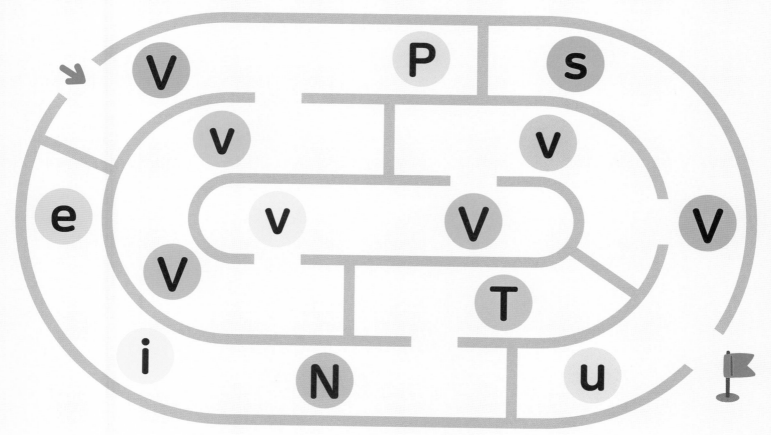

Ww

Splish, splash, Whale.

Look and color, grey for W and blue for w.

W is for 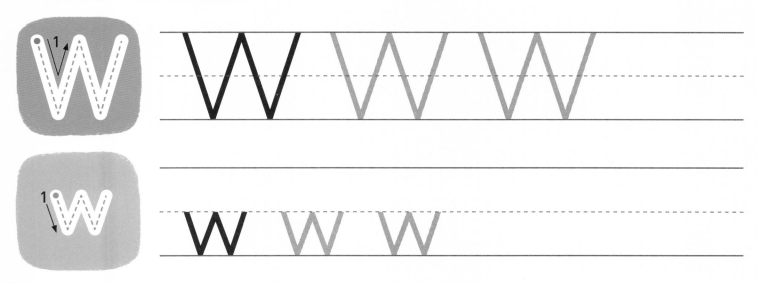 whale.

- Read and write.

W W W W

w w w

- Match the correct big letter and small letter.

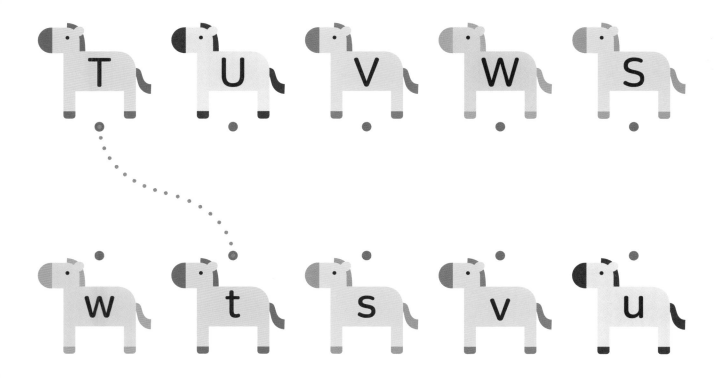

T U V W S

w t s v u

Here is the animal band.

Look and stick the letter X and x.

X is for 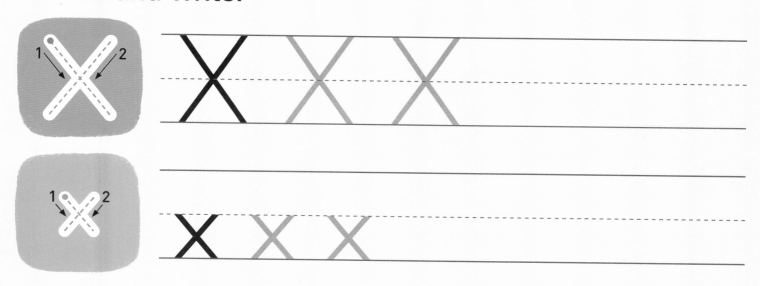 xylophone.

- Read and write.

- Find and circle the wrong letter pairs.

Yy

Move, move! Carry the yogurt.
Look and stick the letter Y and y.

Y is for  yogurt.

- Read and write.

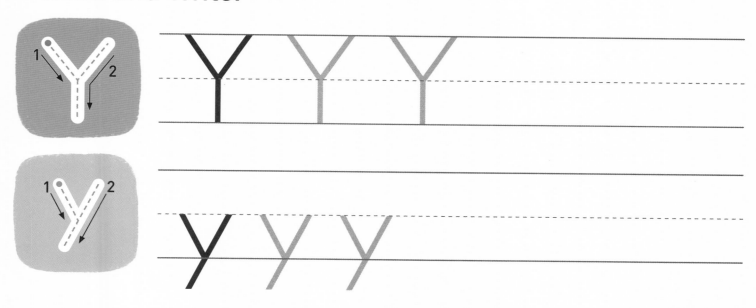

- Draw a line following the letter Y and y from start.

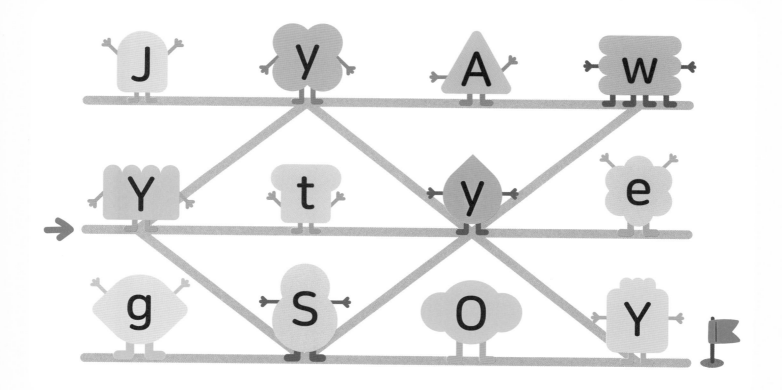

Zz Run, Zebra! Run away!

Look and stick the letter Z and z.

Z is for  zebra.

● Read and write.

Z Z Z Z

z z z z

● Circle the letter Z and z.

a   Z   u   S

B   K   z   d

z   W   i   Z

Picture Alphabet

apple

butterfly

cake

duck

egg

frog

giraffe

hat

ice cream

Aa Aa

Bb Bb

Cc Cc

Dd Dd

Ee Ee

Ff Ff

Gg Gg

Hh Hh

Ii Ii

54

jacket

J j J j

kite

K k K k

ladybird

L l L l

milk

M m M m

necklace

N n N n

orange

O o O o

pumpkin

P p P p

queen

Q q Q q

robot

R r R r

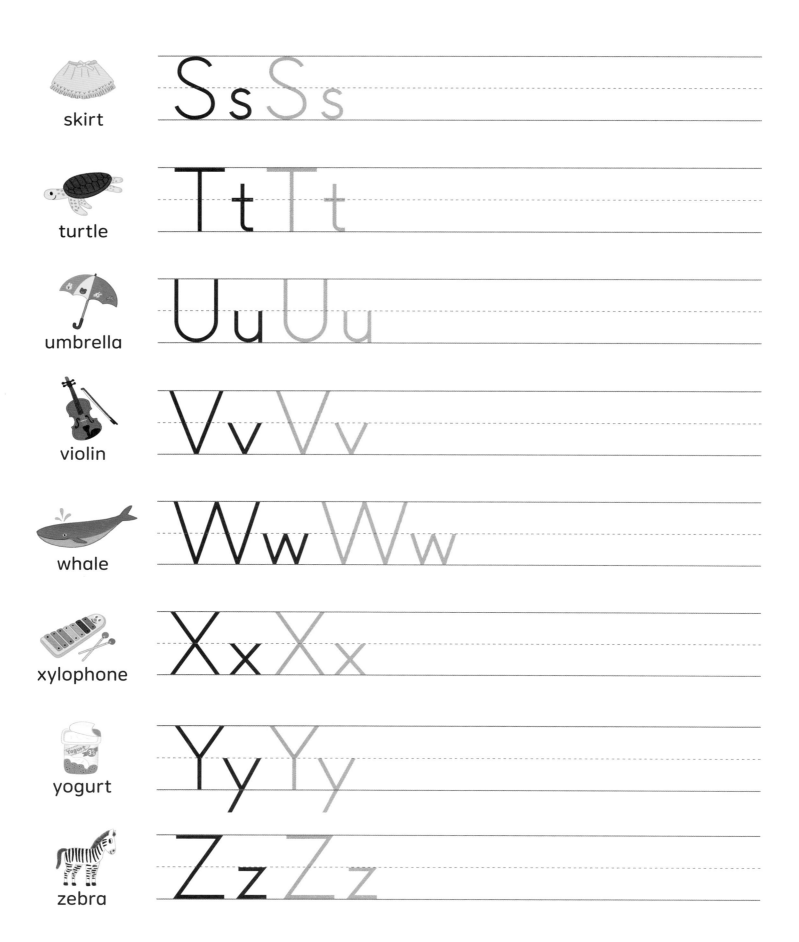

skirt   S s S s

turtle   T t T t

umbrella   U u U u

violin   V v V v

whale   W w W w

xylophone   X x X x

yogurt   Y y Y y

zebra   Z z Z z

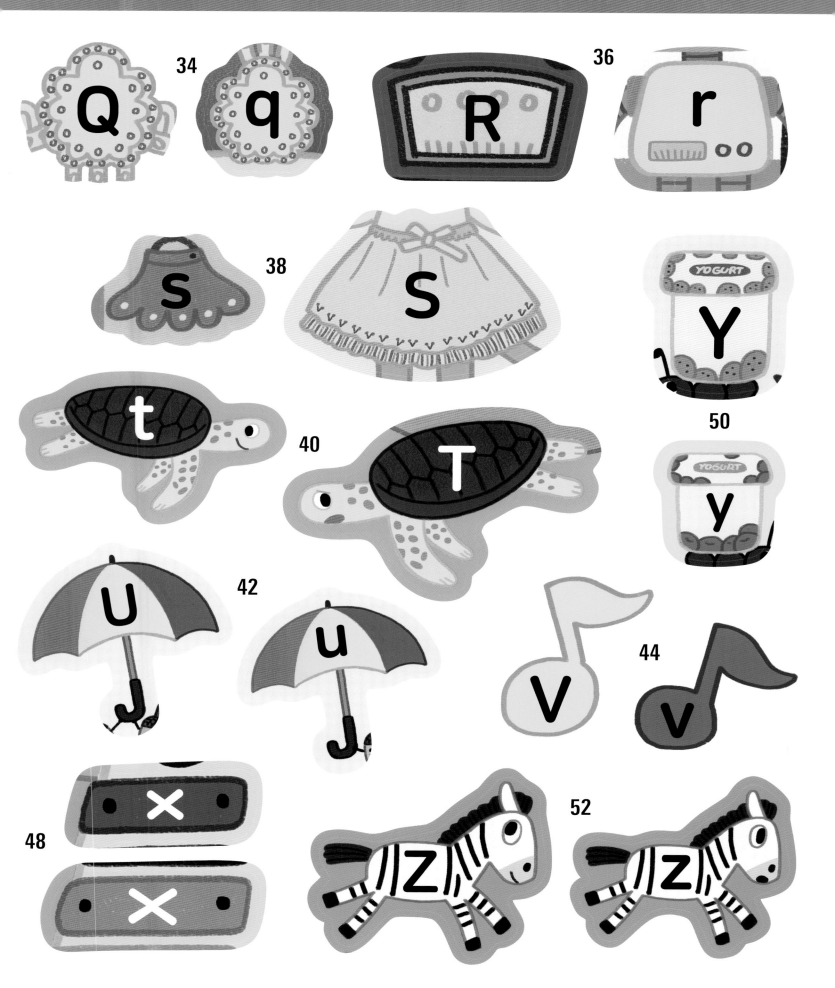